Francesco Jodice

WHAT WE WANT

Landscape as a projection of people's desires

Francesco Jodice   Concept
Luca Molinari   Editor
Paola Tognon   Project supervisor
Meris Angioletti   Project coordinator
Ildebrando Tosi   Art director
Giorgio Tentolini   Graphic Designer
Giovanna Silva   Research
Lindsay Harris   Translations
Lifesaver   Graphic
Mario Govino [studio G&R]   Prints
Arscolor   Enlargements

I am grateful to the following people without whom this project would not have been possible
Stefano Boeri   Luca Molinari   Ildebrando Tosi   Paola Tognon   Meris Angioletti
Davide Di Maggio   Natalina Remotti   Alessandro Seno   Valerio Tazzetti
Anna Rosa and Giovanni Cotroneo   Magda and Rocco Mangia   Multiplicity

This book has been made possible by the generous support of
Galleria Seno   Milan
Mudimadue   Berlin
Photo&Contemporary   Turin
Spazio Erasmus Brera   Milan

Thanks to
Giovanni La Varra   Maki Gherzi   Kal Karman   Vincenzo Castella   Gabriele Basilico   Renato Barbato
Alessandro Cimmino   Lindsay Harris   Giovanna Silva   Giorgio Tentolini   Anna Detheridge   Filippo Maggia
Patrizia Sandretto Re Rebaudengo   Chiara Coronelli   Luca Beatrice   Roberta Valtorta   Andrea Lissoni   Claudia Zanfi

Thanks for *A social landscape: a contribution of projects* to
Artway of thinking   Stefano Boeri   Rachaporn Choochuey and Stefano Mirti
Fabrizio Gallanti and Francisca Insulza   Gruppo A12   Sandi Hilal and Alessandro Petti   Armin Linke   Multiplicity
Hans Ulrich Obrist and Cedric Price   John Palmesino   Stalker   Torolab

My work is dedicated to Sebastiano, Barbara, Angela & Mimmo Jodice

First published in Italy in 2004 by
Skira Editore S.p.A.
Palazzo Casati Stampa
via Torino 61
20123 Milano
Italy
www.skira.net

© 2004 Francesco Jodice
© 2004 Skira editore
© 2004 the authors for their texts and illustrations

Printed and bound in Italy. First edition
ISBN 88-8491-971-1

Distributed in North America and Latin America by Rizzoli International Publications, Inc. through St. Martin's Press, 175 Fifth Avenue, New York, NY 10010.
Distributed elsewhere in the world by Thames and Hudson Ltd., 181a High Holborn, London WC1V 7QX, United Kingdom.

Projects by:

Social landscape has always evolved in a way that is more or less autochthonous, with little regard for political or government strategies concerning the territory. Recently there has been a noticeable change. People have become more conscious of the fact that the environment in which we live is at our own disposal. This recent condition has sharpened our ability to 'perform' and transform spaces, effectively creating a landscape that exists as a projection of our own desires. The accumulation of these actions —repeated infinitely on a large or small scale— allows people to impress their will upon the surrounding territory by transforming the shape and significance of these places. This catalogue of seemingly casual gestures often creates an impact that can be considered deliberate, almost political, as it presents a sort of *occupation* of spaces, albeit prefabricated and temporary. *What We Want* is a compelling project of photographs, accounts and maps that describe an urban geography modified by new pioneers. The images in this book also reflect upon the changes necessary in our way of seeing to perceive a landscape that is no longer comprehensible from a single point of view. This multiple perspective is accentuated by the use of different artistic genres and materials, such as topographical and reportage photography, conceptual artworks, maps, and writings. By comparing phenomena that occur in different parts of the world and focusing in on things that are both close and far away, the work allows us to look at our surroundings in an almost scientific or entomological way. The visual elements of this project, which in part abandon the convention of organising an inventory of human experience, attempt to reveal the parallel reflection between the things we look at and the way we look at them.

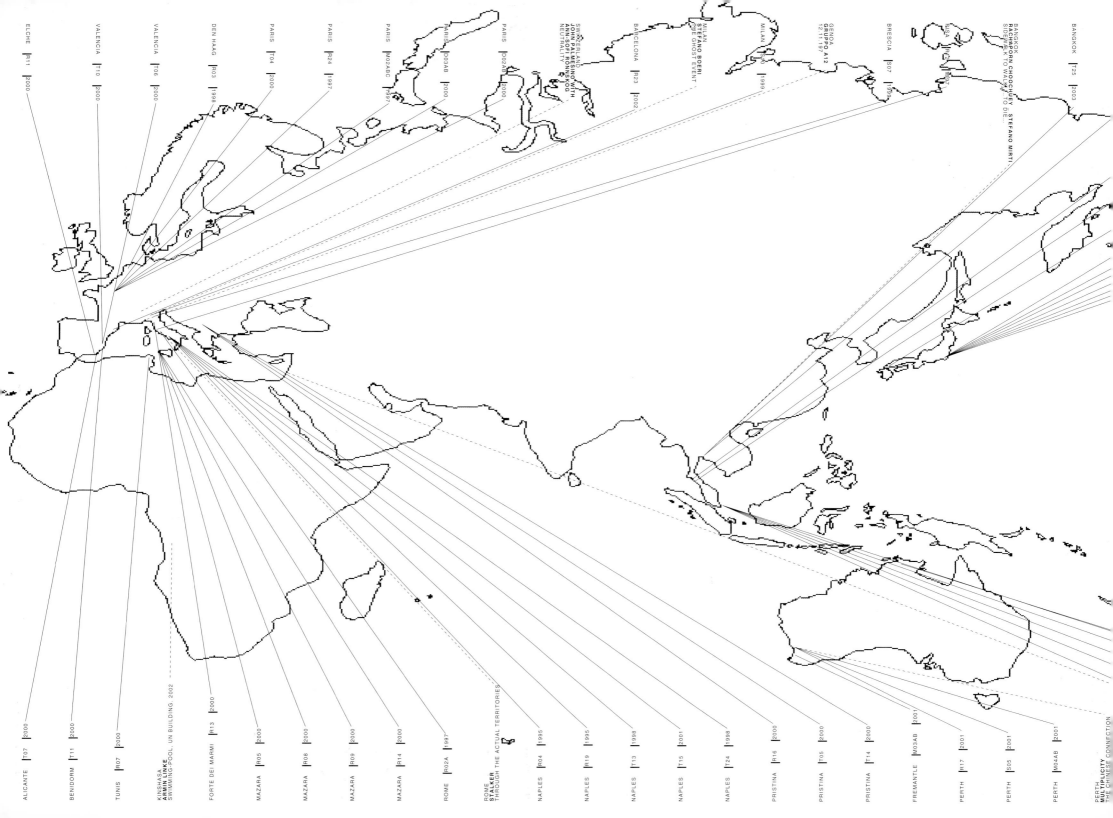

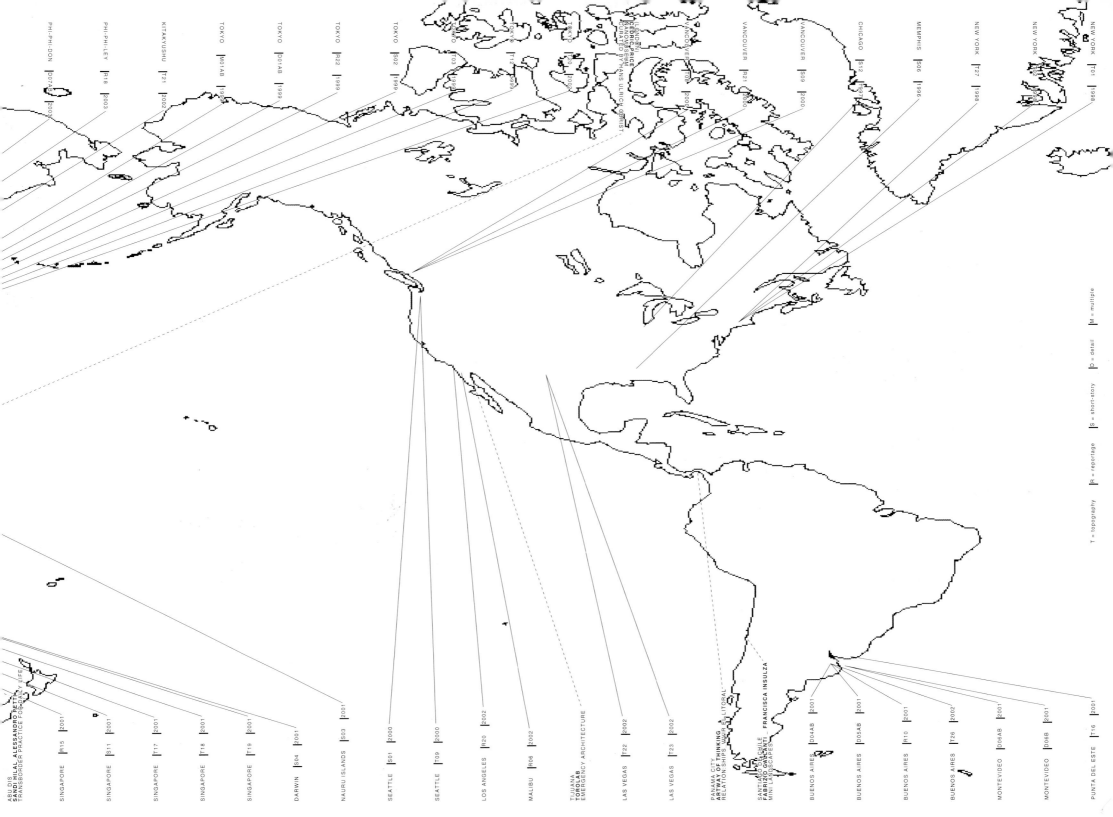

PHI-PHI-DON |D07AB |2003
PHI-PHI-LEY |R18 |2003
KITAKYUSHU |T21 |2002
TOKYO |M01AB |1999
TOKYO |D01AB |1999
TOKYO |R22 |1999
TOKYO |S02 |1999

VANCOUVER
VANCOUVER |R21 |2000
VANCOUVER |S09 |2000
CHICAGO |S12 |1997
MEMPHIS |S06 |1996
NEW YORK |T27 |1998
NEW YORK
NEW YORK |T01 |1998

(LLOUD(R))
CEDRIC PRICE
NANOMUSEUM
CURATED BY HANS ULRICH OBRIST

T = topography |S = short-story |p = detail
|R = reportage |M = multiple

ABU DIS
SANDI HILAL ALESSANDRO PETTI
TRANSBORDER PRACTICE FOR DAILY LIFE
SINGAPORE |R15 |2001
SINGAPORE |S11 |2001
SINGAPORE |T17 |2001
SINGAPORE |T18 |2001
SINGAPORE |T19 |2001
DARWIN |S04 |2001
NAURU ISLANDS |S03 |2001
SEATTLE |S01 |2000
SEATTLE |T09 |2000
LOS ANGELES |R20 |2002
MALIBU |R06 |2002
TIJUANA
TOROLAB
EMERGENCY ARCHITECTURE
LAS VEGAS |T22 |2002
LAS VEGAS |T23 |2002
PANAMA CITY
ARTWAY OF THINKING
RELATION SHIPS W/R EL LITORAL
SANTIAGO DE CHILE
FABRIZIO GALLANTI   FRANCISCA INSULZA
MINI LANDSCAPES
BUENOS AIRES |D04AB |2001
BUENOS AIRES |D05AB |2001
BUENOS AIRES |R10 |2001
BUENOS AIRES |T26 |2002
MONTEVIDEO |D06AB |2001
MONTEVIDEO |D06B |2001
PUNTA DEL ESTE |T16 |2001

Landscape as a projection of people's desires

BUENOS AIRES ‖D04AB ‖2001

I am in the elevator at the King's Inn in Seattle with two travel agents. The first travel agent tells the other one about this guy in Mexico who owns a lot of cottages there. All the interiors are in Old English style. Every comfort included. The second travel agent asks, "Does he have a website with pictures of each room?" "Yep! One picture, one room!" "Then it can be done."

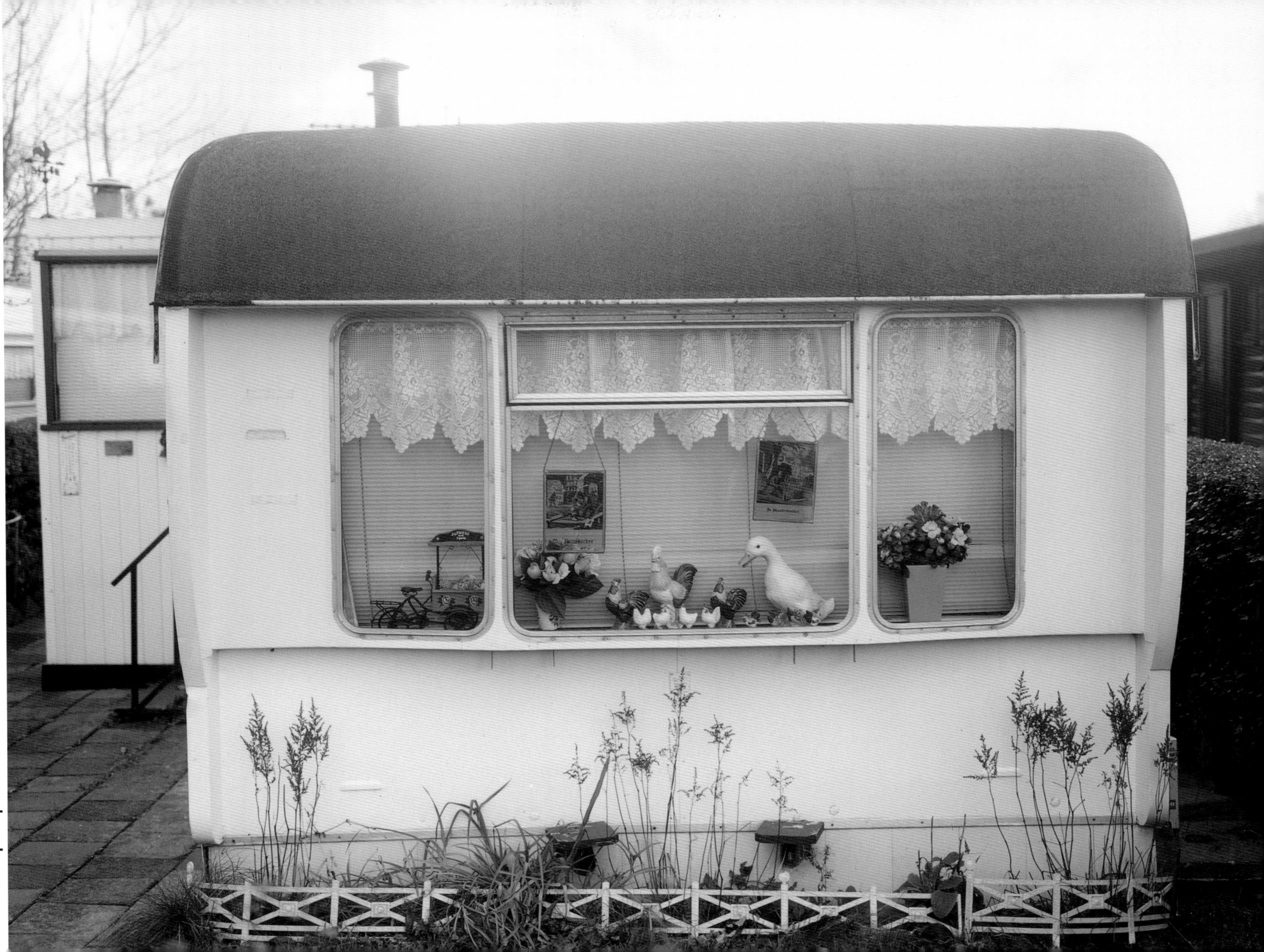

DEN HAAG | R03 | 1998

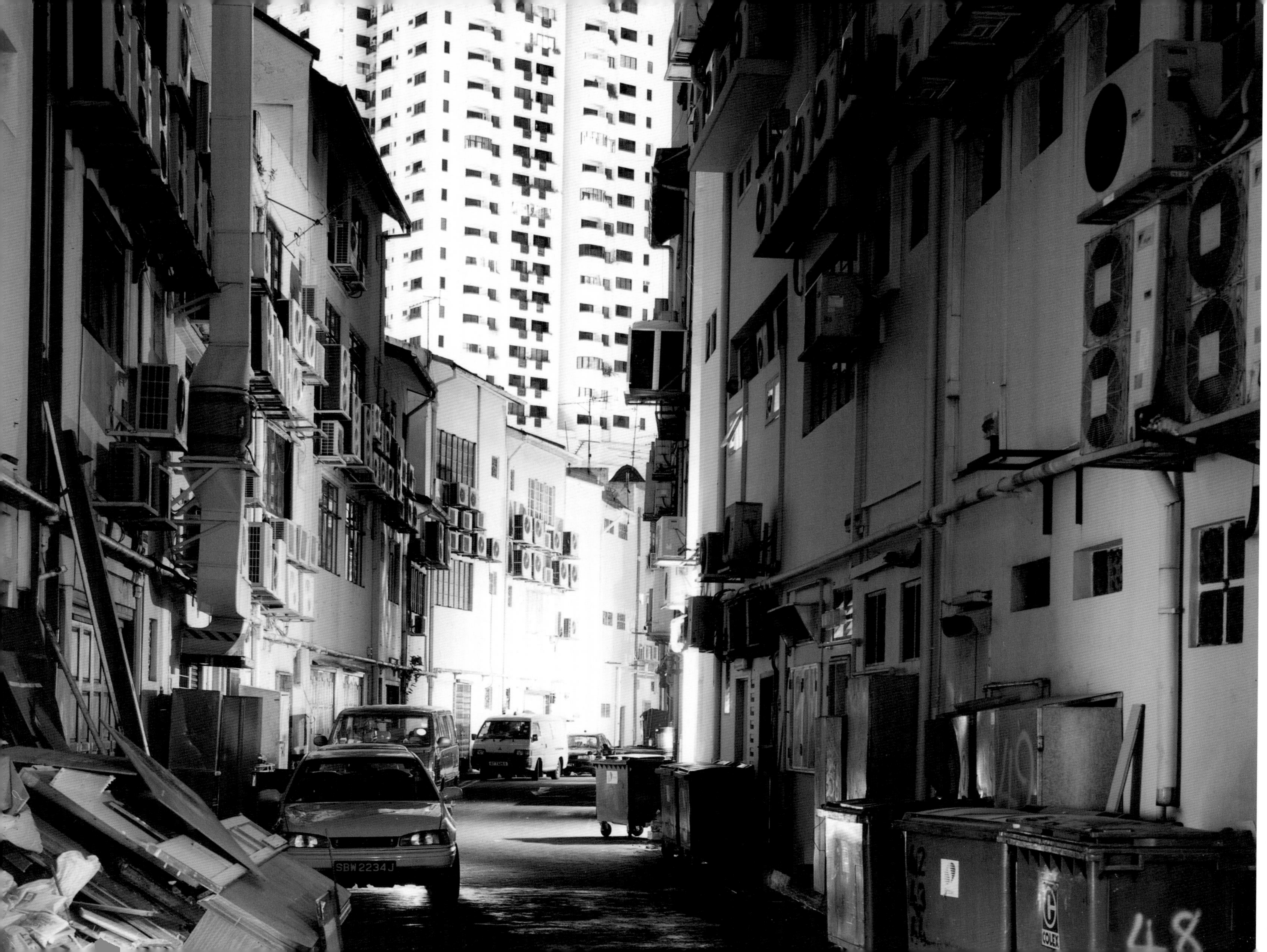

SINGAPORE | T19 | 2001

Last November, a boy died after taking XTC at a rave in a forest somewhere near a wealthy, northern Italian city. The police only discovered by accident that the rave was part of a huge European tour. Information about the tour had been distributed through various websites on the Internet. Small trucks armed with electrical generators provided stages and amplification. Pills and drugs followed through the usual channels. The rave was held one night in a forest not far from a highway exit leading to a city of 35,000 people. 40,000 ravers took part. If no one had died, no one would have known anything.

I'm in a phone booth in Roppongi, Tokyo. The lady on the phone keeps telling me something in Japanese that I can't understand. A second lady enters the phone booth and asks me in terrible English if I'm in fact English. I tell her I'm Italian. She seems disappointed. Like most Roppongi nightwalkers, she's looking for native English speakers to take her out to dinner so she can learn perfect English. Before disappearing, she makes my long-distance calling card work.

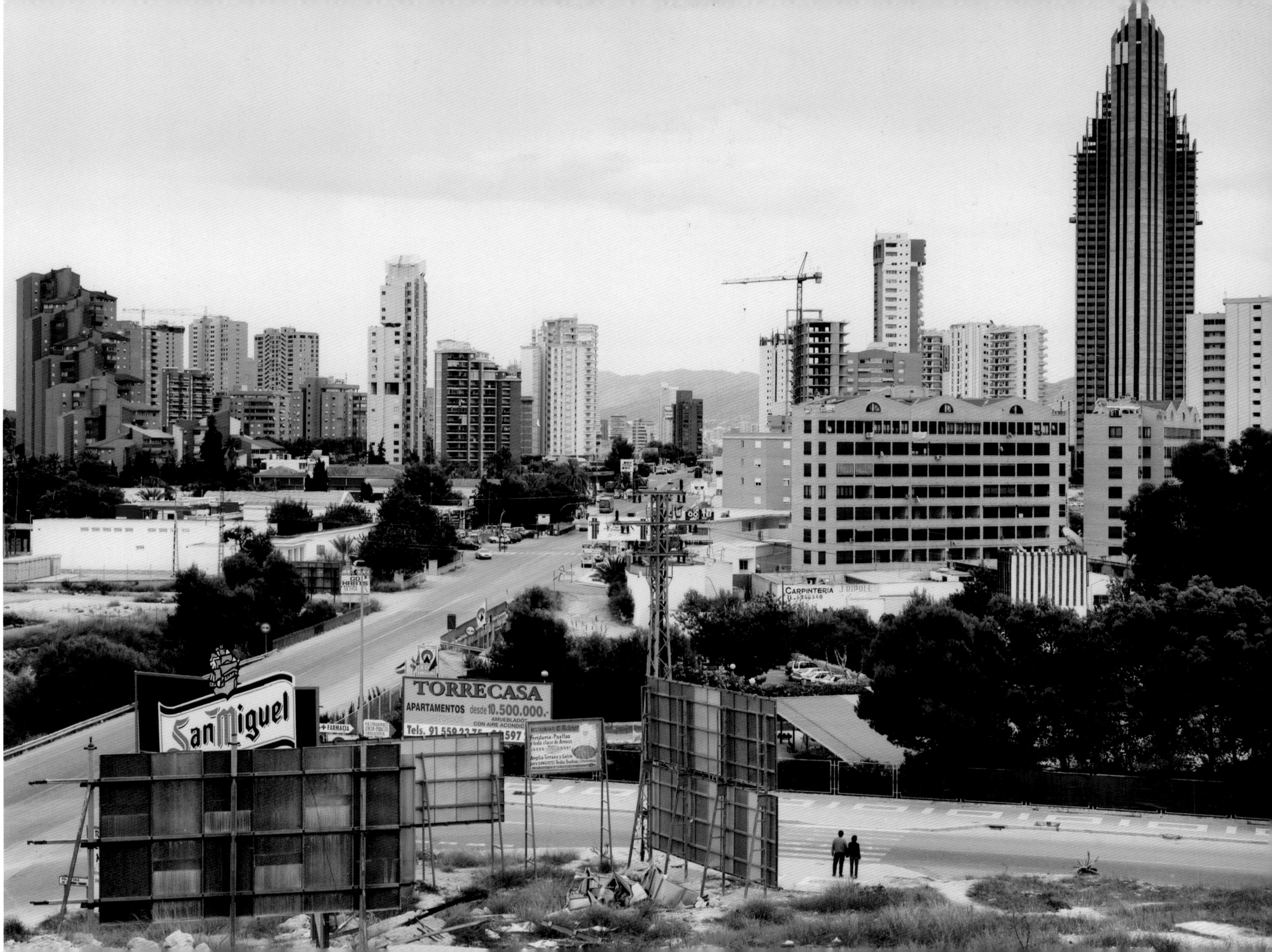

BENIDORM | T11 | 2000

Mr. Keng, our taxi driver, says people paid a lot of money for these apartments because they wanted a view of the sea from their balconies, a precious thing to have in Singapore. Ten years later, somebody has built new high-rises in front of them. These new apartments will be very expensive because now they own the view of the sea.

NAPLES | T13 | 1998

Christine says that the refugees are kept on the Nauru Islands. Most came by boat from Southeast Asia, some came from Afghanistan. "The Australian government is paying a lot of money to keep them there," she says. "We use landscape to imprison people."

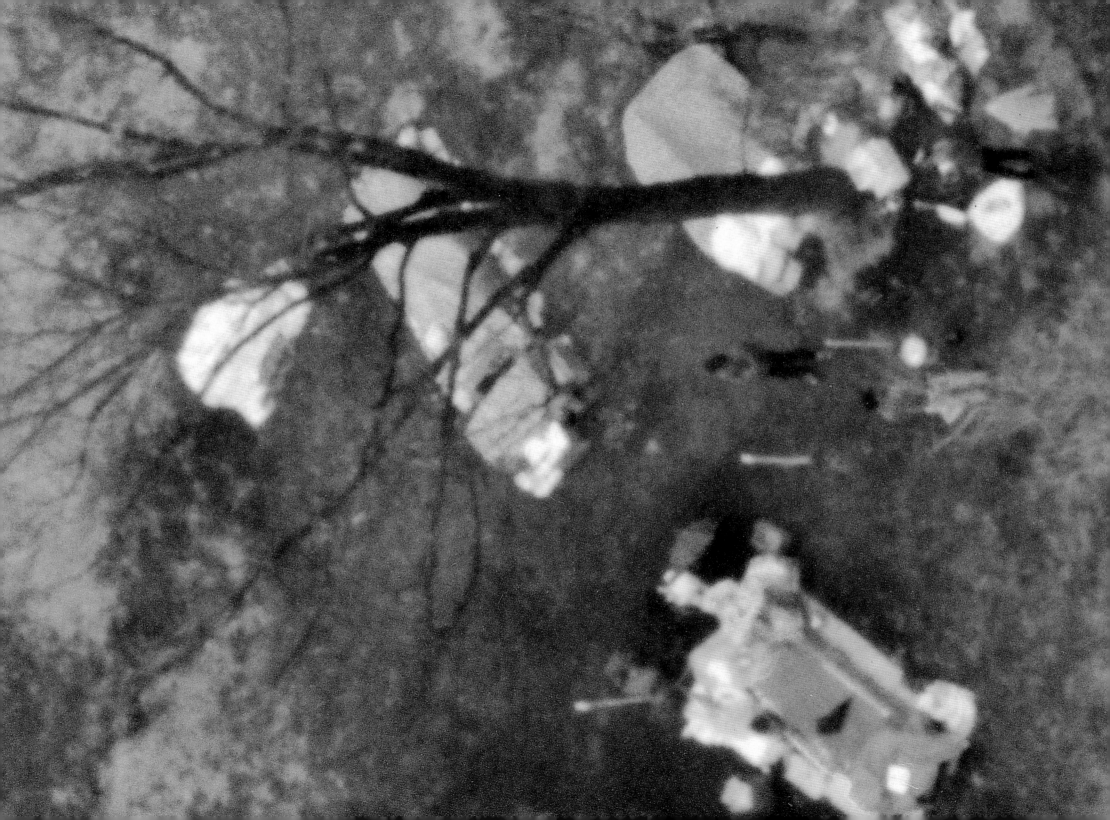

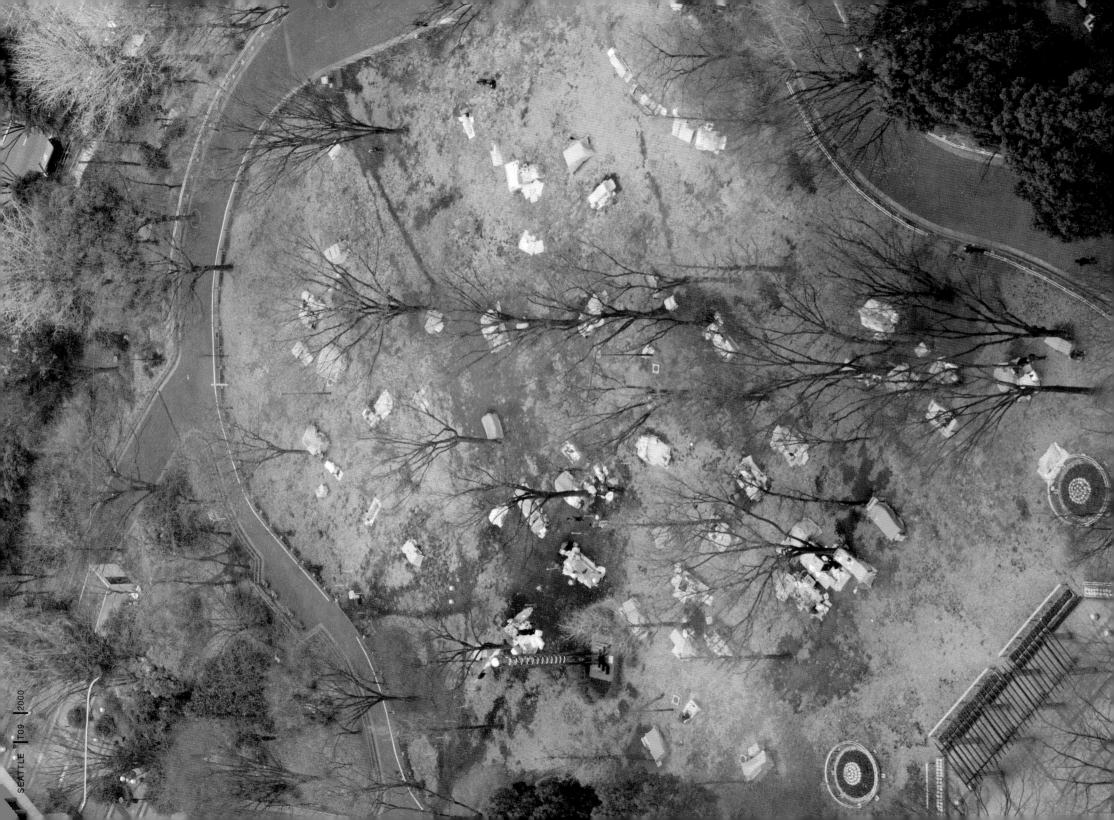

BANGKOK | T24 | 2003

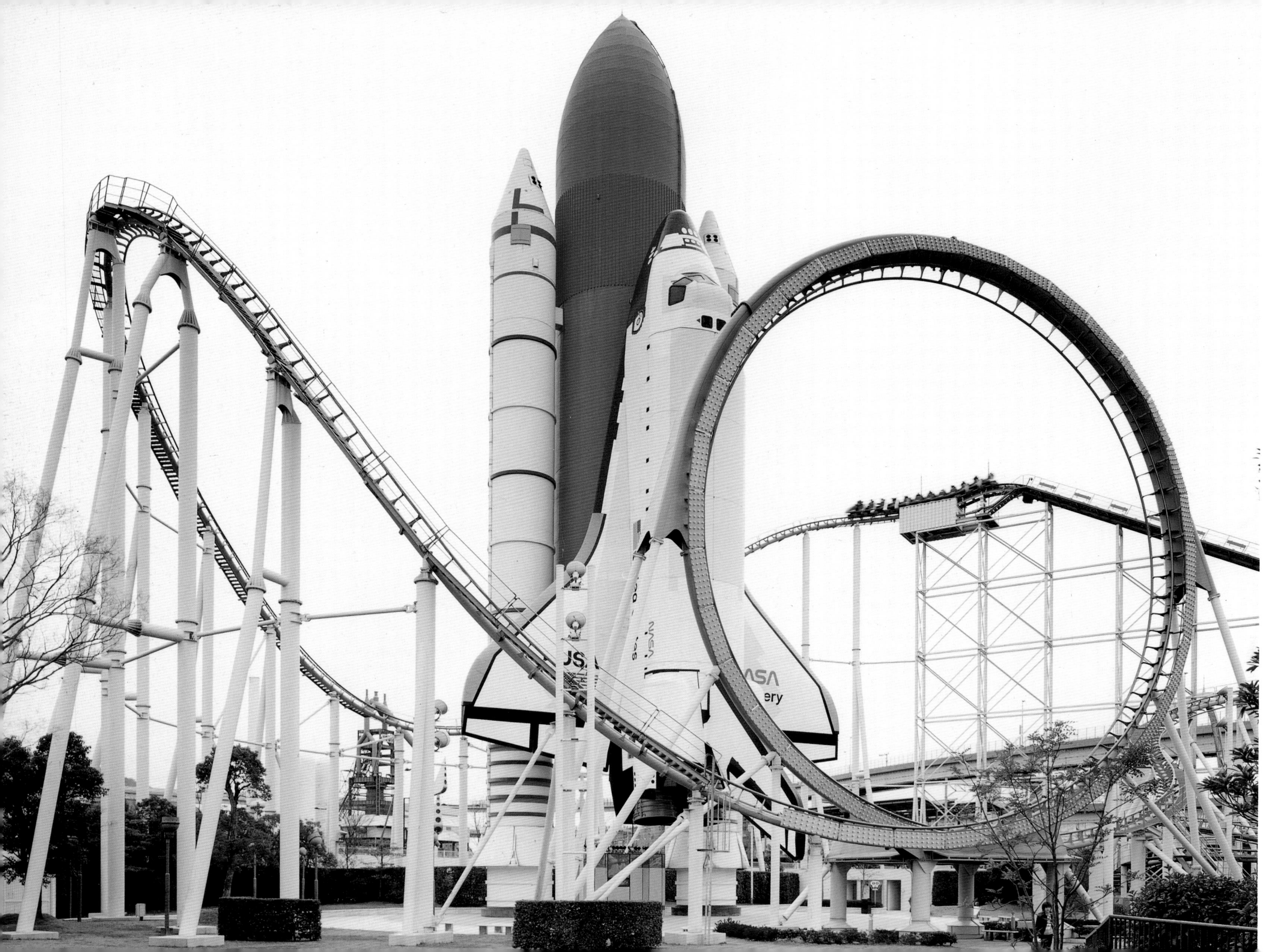

KITAKYUSHU | T21 | 2002

Simon tells us about this friend of his in Darwin. He drives an ambulance. He has nothing to do the whole week. Then on Friday the aborigines get paid. That's when the trouble starts.They all get drunk, then his friend has to work like crazy for 48 hours.

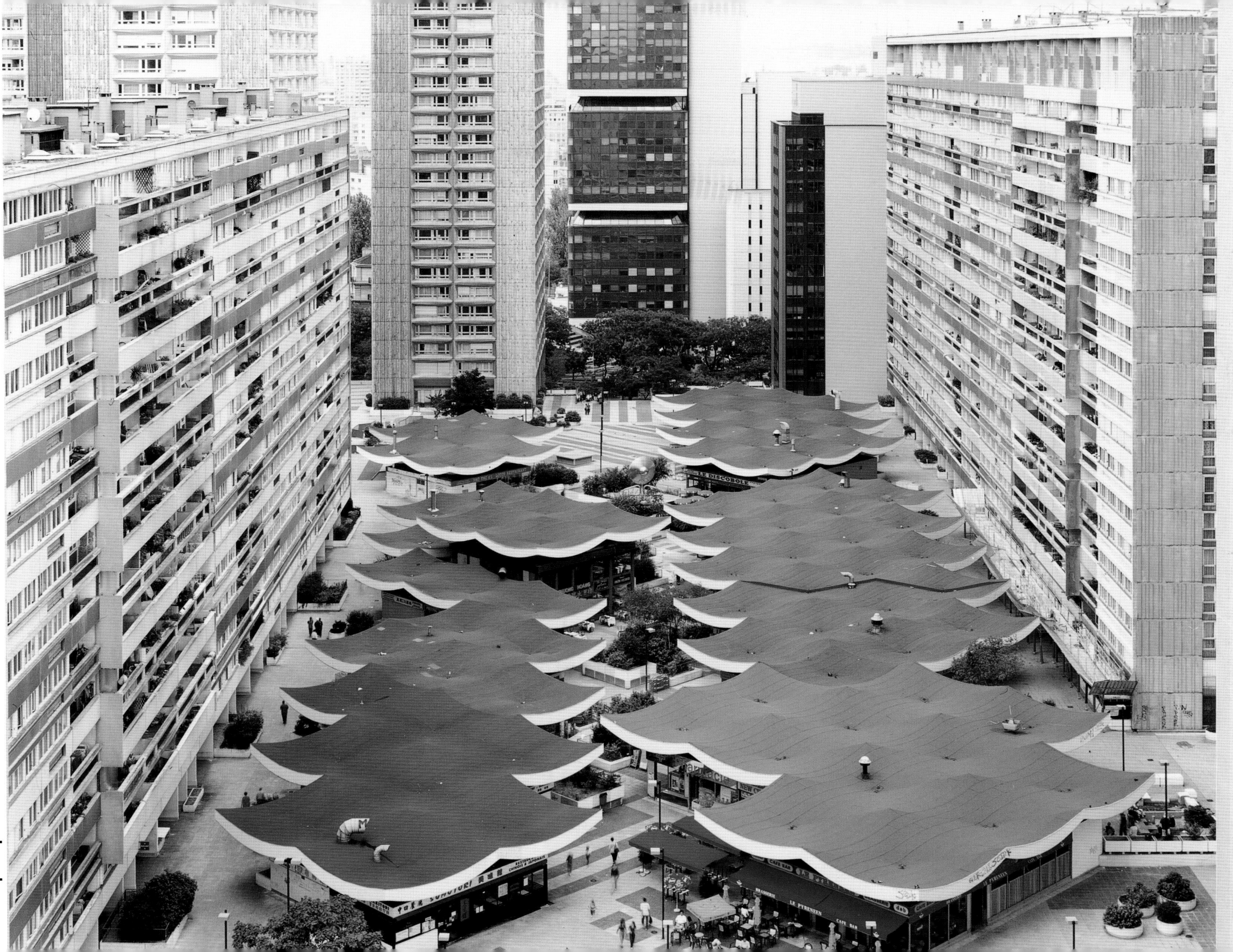

PARIS | T04 | 2000

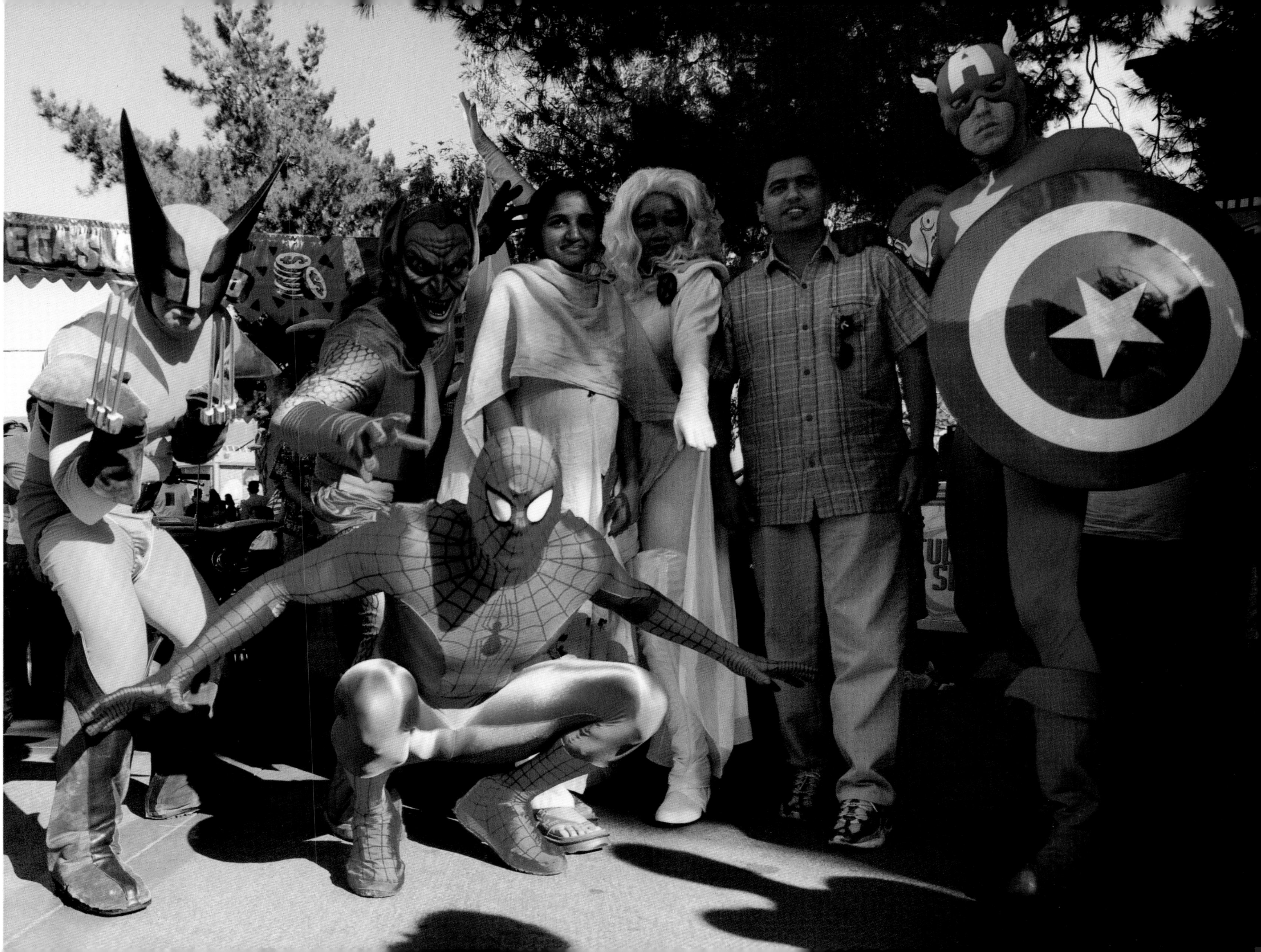

LOS ANGELES | R20 | 2002

LAURA
GRACIELA
PEREZ REY

BUENOS AIRES | D05AB | 2001

I'm in the backyard of Mister James Chow's house in Perth. He's barbecuing Kangaroo meat. He came to Australia from Malaysia 35 years ago and now owns a small factory making pillows. Some of his raw materials come from China, some from Germany. Mr. Chow tells me he has a partner who's Spanish. "He's a good fella."

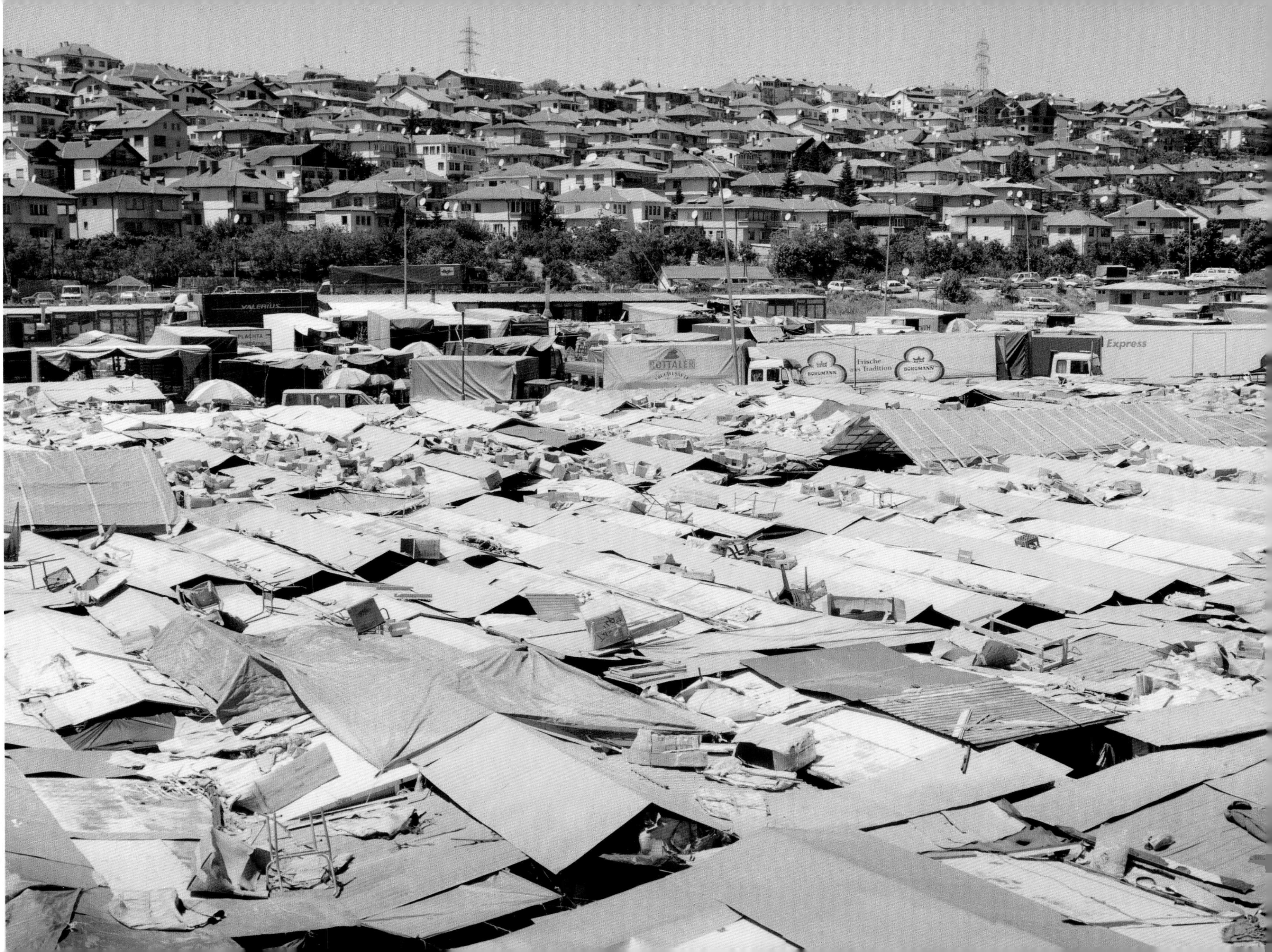

PRISTINA | T05 | 2000

NAPLES   R04   1995

TOKYO |R22 |1999

North Hollywood has been re-born in Vancouver. That's where Los Angeles is making today's movies because it's cheaper than in L.A. and, as a city councillor tells me, "The great thing about Vancouver is that you can make this place look like anywhere!"

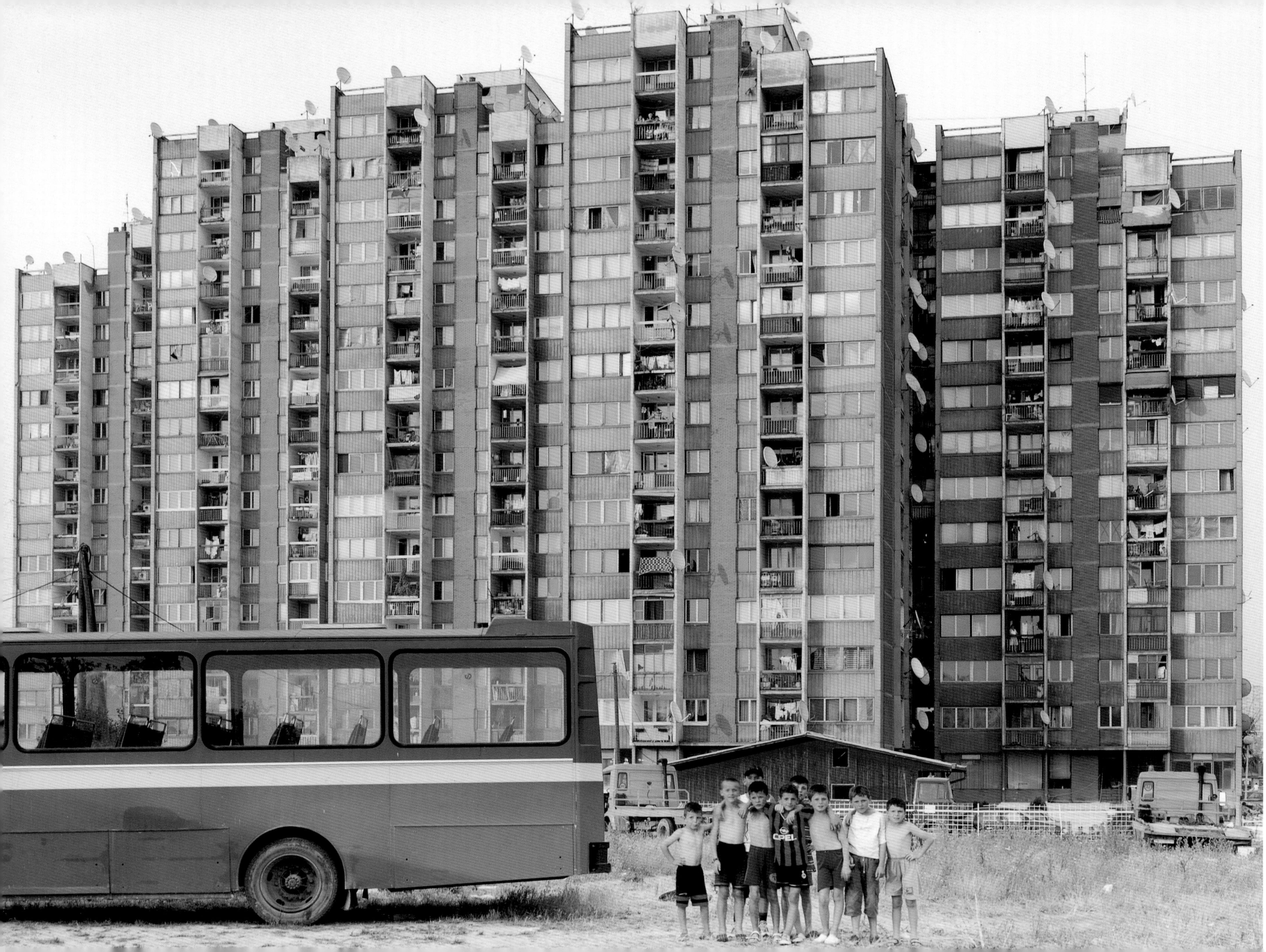

PRISTINA | T14 | 2000

47 Rome

65 Mexico

70 Sapporo

75 Athènes

There are these two guys sitting at the bar. They're both quite drunk and speaking to each other in confidential tones. One guy, a real estate agent, hands the other a brochure. The brochure shows a piece of land glowing warm in the sunshine; slogans and illustrations allude to the beauty of the houses yet to be built. The client looks through the brochure, and the agent says: "Want to show you something. It may say something to you, it may not. I don't know. I don't know anymore."

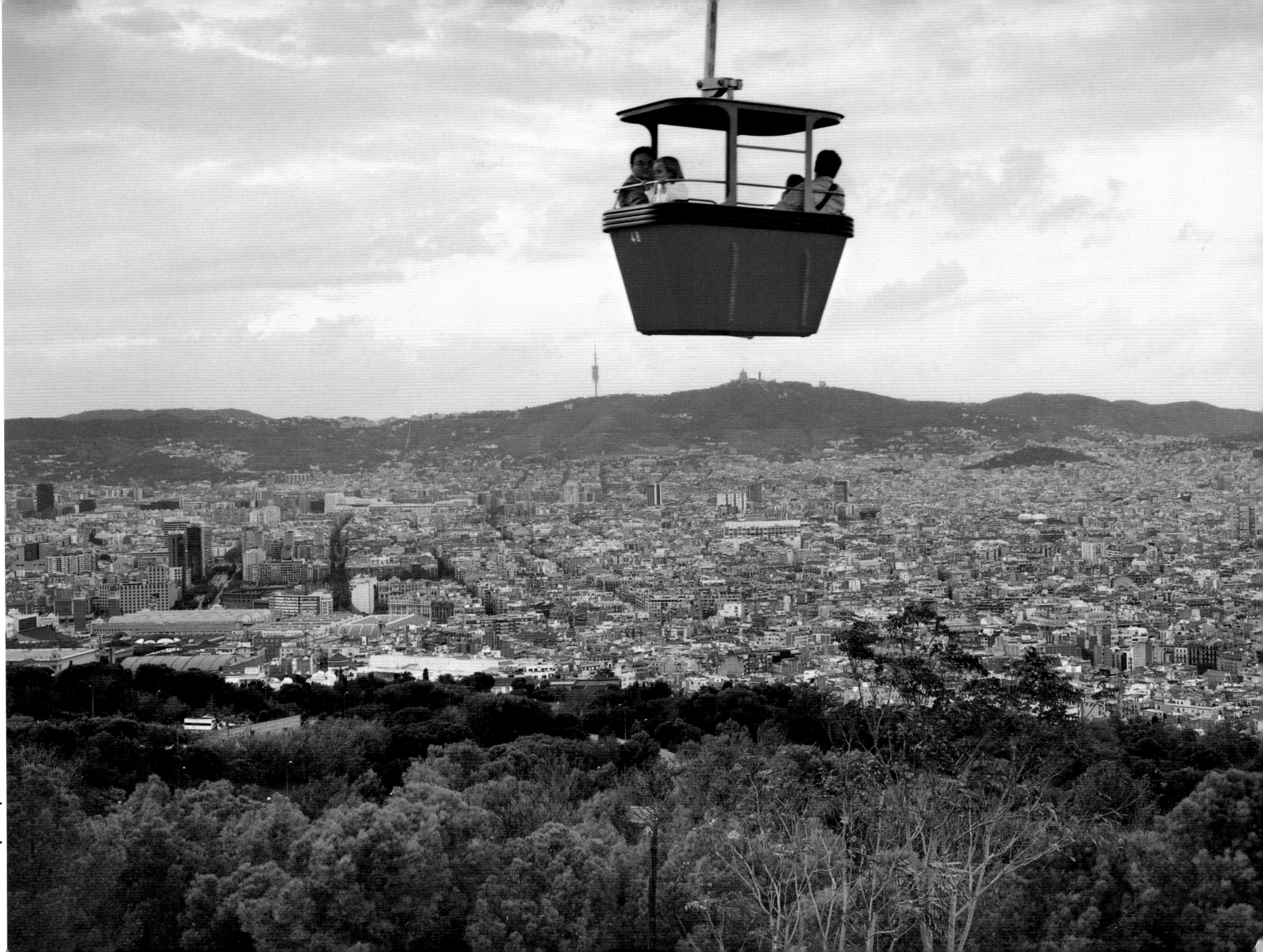

BARCELONA | R23 | 2002

Artway of thinking | Panama City | relation:ships _vivir el litoral

Stefano Boeri | Milan | The ghost event

Rachaporn Choochuey _ Stefano Mirti | Bangkok | Sidewalk to walk, …to eat, …to talk, …to drink, …to buy, …to sell, …to bribe, …to relax, …to sleep, …to love, …to die…

(Illustrated by Superlover: Piaypong Bhumichitra, Chuti Srisanguanvila)

Fabrizio Gallanti _ Francisca Insulza | Santiago de Chile | Mini landscapes

Sandi Hilal _ Alessandro Petti | Abu Dis (occupied Palestinian territories) | Transborder practice for daily life

Gruppo A12 | Genoa | 12.11.1972

Armin Linke | Kinshasa Congo | Swimming-pool, UN building, 2002

Multiplicity | Perth | The Chinese connection

Cedric Price | (London) | Nanomuseum | Curated by Hans Ulrich Obrist

John Palmesino with Ann-Sofi Rönnskog | Switzerland | Neutrality

Stalker | Rome | Through the actual territories

Torolab | Tijuana | Emergency architecture

122

A social landscape: a contribution of projects

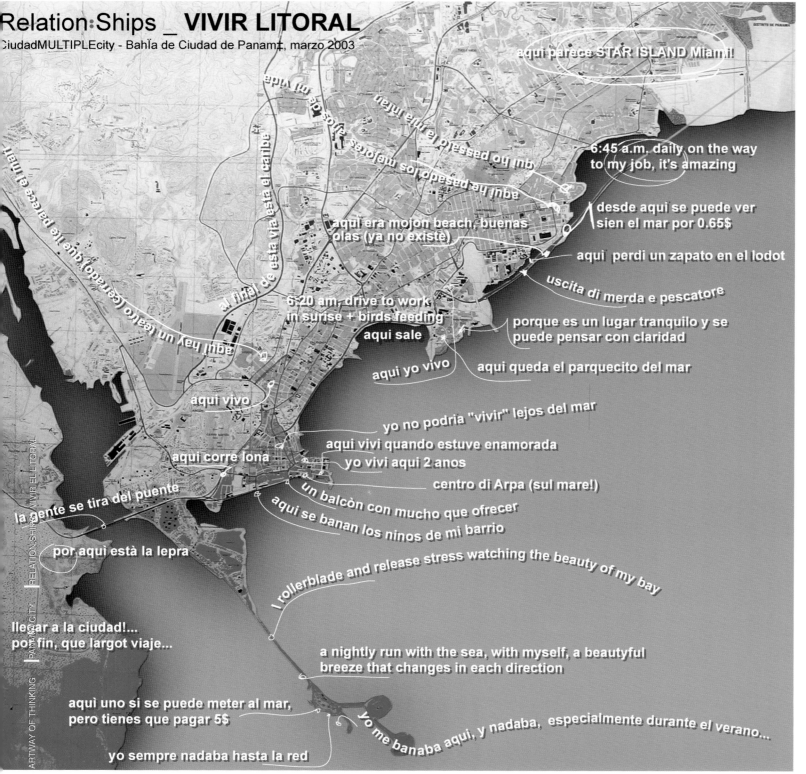

Relation:Ships _ **VIVIR LITORAL**

CiudadMULTIPLEcity - Bahía de Ciudad de Panamá, marzo 2003

aquí parece STAR ISLAND Miami!

6:45 a.m. daily on the way to my job, it's amazing

desde aquí se puede ver sien el mar por 0.65$

aquí era mojon beach, buenas olas (ya no existe)

aquí perdi un zapato en el lodot

uscita di merda e pescatore

6:20 am, drive to work in surise + birds feeding aquí sale

porque es un lugar tranquilo y se puede pensar con claridad

aquí yo vivo

aquí queda el parquecito del mar

aquí vivo

yo no podria "vivir" lejos del mar

aquí corre lona

aquí vivi quando estuve enamorada

yo vivi aqui 2 anos

centro di Arpa (sul mare!)

un balcòn con mucho que ofrecer

aqui se banan los ninos de mi barrio

la gente se tira del puente

I rollerblade and release stress watching the beauty of my bay

por aquí està la lepra

llegar a la ciudad!... por fin, que largot viaje...

a nightly run with the sea, with myself, a beautyful breeze that changes in each direction

aquì uno si se puede meter al mar, pero tienes que pagar 5$

yo me banaba aqui, y nadaba, especialmente durante el verano...

yo sempre nadaba hasta la red

INVITACIÓN
Aceptamos con entusiasmo la invitación a participar en ciudadMULTIPLE con un proyecto sobre la identidad de la ciudad de Panamá, involucrando a artistas y profesionales panameños. Vemos el arte como un proceso creativo colectivo, que debe desenvolverse dentro del contexto social. Así, el artista se convierte en traductor de un sueño vital y común, aunque no manifiesto.

PANAMÁ VISTA DESDE FUERA
Teníamos una "idea de Panamá", un prejuicio. El nombre "Panamá" –desde fuera, desde Europa– refiere en primer lugar a un canal, después a la flota comercial más grande del mundo, después a una nación y, ulteriormente, a una ciudad.

PANAMÁ VISTA CON OJOS PANAMEÑOS
Llegamos a la ciudad de Panamá en agosto de 2002. Para verla con ojos limpios pedimos a un grupo de panameños (arquitectos, urbanistas, músicos, escritores, psicólogos, etc.) que nos prestaran sus ojos para observar la ciudad, para conocer su alma. En los primeros dos días exploramos Panamá en un gran mapa. En este los panameños señalaban sus itinerarios temáticos personales, que recorrían diversos paisajes urbanos y sociales. En los diez días sucesivos estas personas nos acompañaron en los recorridos físicos de sus itinerarios; encontramos a través de ellos otros profesionales panameños que nos transmitieron sus visiones e ideas sobre la ciudad. Al narrarnos su propia ciudad, los panameños repensaron sus raíces, advirtiendo cómo se reconocían a sí mismos, cómo pertenecían (o no) a ella. Lo que sucedió en realidad fue que durante esta exploración los panameños miraron con ojos distintos su propia ciudad: al infringir la mirada habitual, veían con los ojos y la curiosidad de un extranjero. Un tema emergió con fuerza: Panamá tiene raíces en el mar. Pero al mismo tiempo la vida cotidiana de esta ciudad ha establecido una relación difícil y contradictoria con el mar, con la bahía y con el litoral que la recorre. La historia civil y el desarrollo urbano de Panamá parecen haber olvidado esta elemental raíz energética, esta profunda identidad. En la entrada del Mercado del marisco hay un letrero que dice "NO LE DES LA ESPALDA AL MAR". Recogemos esta voz para hacer de ella el mensaje principal del proyecto porque es esta la síntesis de todas las voces escuchadas, de nuestro sentir unido al de nuestros compañeros panameños de viaje.

ENFOQUE DEL PROYECTO
Relation:Ships _ VIVIR EL LITORAL busca que resurja esta conciencia, este profundo pero olvidado sentido de pertenencia, esta relación vital con el mar. Pretende decir en voz alta –la voz colectiva recogida durante el proceso– "NO LE DES LA ESPALDA AL MAR". El PROCESO _ recolectando atenciones hacia la bahía. Desde agosto 2002, junto al grupo de trabajo panameño, hemos recogido historias, testimonios, puntos de vista, imágenes, sonidos de la bahía de Panamá. El proceso colectivo siguió hasta el 28 de marzo 2003. Continuaron los encuentros con panameños de distintos ámbitos, las conversaciones, el acopio de relatos vividos, escenarios posibles, imágenes, sonidos. Continúa la atención diseminada y puntual hacia la bahía que culminó con el evento público previsto para el sábado 29 de marzo.

VIVIR EL LITORAL _ ritual de reconciliación
La culminación del proceso, el ritual colectivo de reconciliación entre la ciudad y el mar constituyó el momento participativo más intenso con la bahía. Un momento de atención colectiva hacia la bahía y lo que esta representa para la ciudad y el mar. Un encuentro con esas comunidades confinadas y poco visibles que viven día a día la bahía. Se utilizó la forma del ritual como foco de atención que se mueve desde lo personal (encuentros, entrevistas) hasta lo trans-personal, lo colectivo. El ritual operó como una especie de acelerador o acumulador de atención sobre la bahía, de energía con la cual saldar la relación entre la ciudad y el mar. Vivir el litoral, el espacio / tiempo del ritual, inició a las 7.30 de la noche en el Parque de Punta Paitilla. Como una "sirena" la Banda del Hogar hizo una llamada a la gente de la ciudad para que se acercara al mar. A las 8.00 p.m. una palabra-clave susurrada al oído abrió las puertas al espacio de la reconciliación. La música: un crecer de sonidos, recopilados a lo largo del litoral, se convirtió en música y luego en cantos. Se proyectaron imágenes de la bahía y de las comunidades que viven en ella. Adquirieron una voz las historias y los puntos de vista recopilados entre los panameños. Una convivencia medió el encuentro.

VISIONES

The bay woke up, she was sick. There was the sun, trying to wake her. There was the city, ready to embrace her. Waiting, waiting, sun, hot and city waiting. The bay woke up and she was sick.

ENCUENTROS

"Bad news," said one little boy to his summer friend. "They say Bahia's getting worse, short of breath, no oxygen, in her lungs. They called one doctor to heal her, but he cost too much.

PANAMÁ VISTA CON OJOS PANAMEÑOS

The fisherman took off his hat, and looked out to the seas beyond his boat. "Bahia, I know you're sleeping, perhaps still kind of weak. But there's no reason to be ailing anymore. We've decided to give you relief."

VIVIR EL LITORAL _ ritual de reconciliación

Finally, she woke up, and Bahia said with a rejuvenated voice, "I'm so glad to hear your collective call. I want to return to you all. I like meeting people from all over the world."

'The Ghost Event.' (The propagation of a ghost event.) In 1968, the 'Triennale di Milan' entrusted Giancarlo De Carlo with the organisation of the 14th International Exhibition. De Carlo chose a theme that was for the period, radical and not a contemporary issue. 'Il Grande Numero' [The Big Number] was critical of both the proliferation of individual consumerism, and ideological radicalisation with the homogenisation of behaviour, which had already begun to bolster and institutionalise the fledgling revolutionary movements. 'Grande Numero' –opposed to the mass, movement, class– as the sum of irreducible individuality. 'Grande Numero' –opposed to party politics, avant-garde, organisation– as a 'multitude' of autonomous subjects who share a common choice. 'Grande Numero' –opposed to planning, territorial government, urban law– as an attempt to introduce an anarchical seed of thought into reflection on thecity. 'Grande Numero' –opposed to a city of component parts, monuments, residential areas, public districts, centre/periphery– as a critical vision of the individualistic fragmentation that had, by that time, already begun to characterise the suburban areas of European cities. To illustrate the theme of 'Il Grande Numero' Giancarlo De Carlo called upon some recognised names involved in the international debate, albeit little known in Italy: Soul Bass (who had constructed an immense framework on which to place creativity), the scholar of percetion George Kepes ('the shape of the city at night'), the Archigrams, Peter Smithson, Aldo van Eyck, Arata Isozaki... along with intellectual and artistic Italians such as Marco Zanuso, Albe Steiner, Alberto Rosselli. Surprisingly, however, on the day the exhibition was due to open, architectural students and a group of Milanese artists (who were among those not invited to the exhibition by De Carlo) proceeded to invade and occupy the 'Triennale,' which was seen as an institution of power. The occupation took place after a lengthy discussion with De Carlo outside the 'Palazzo dell'Arte'

of Milan, who attempted to convince them as to the importance of the proposed themes of the exhibition and of the urgency to discuss them. He had little success. This big misunderstanding (or possibly a violent, unconscious intolerance towards such a 'cutting' theme, difficult even for the leaders of the new European Left to accept) lasted for ten days of occupation, destroying almost all of the preparations. At the end of the tenth day the police, called in by the Board of Directors of the Triennale, stormed into the Palazzo dell'Arte, removing the protestors. The 14th Triennale never opened. Nobody, except the caretakers, the invited artists and the protestors, saw the exhibition. Yet, paradoxically, that sophisticated and forward thinking reflection on mass individualism, never even inaugurated, came to have extraordinary success in the years following. Indeed, it was to be a far greater and enduring success than many celebrated exhibitions on an urban theme. Furthermore, today 'Il Grande Numero' appears to be the only code through which it is possible to decipher the new diffused town we see scattered around, and often connecting European cities. The 14th Triennale was, therefore, a kind of 'ghost event' that –as it is for the books that we never read, but hear spoken of so frequently– we have made sense of through notoriety rather than experience. A 'void' so surrounded by rumour, that it became full. The exhibition on 'Il Grande Numero' survived to witness its implosion, largely because the only people to have witnessed it were a group of artists, critics and intellectuals who, with time, became an elite in the world of European culture. On the international circuit, it is ever more frequent to hear it spoken of when people discuss or are looking for new models to represent the contemporary urban condition. Today, without this reflection on 'Il Grande Numero', the town that we live in would appear even more difficult to interpret.

Bangkok

Sidewalk to walk, …to eat, …to talk, …to drink, …to buy, … to sell, …to bribe, …to relax, …to sleep, …to love, …to die…

In Bangkok everything is fluid.
The Chao Praya River is the mother of everything, and from there on everything is tuned on the dark muddy water floating toward the sea.
To explain this concept we chose a specific phenomenon deeply rooted in the use of the public space of the city: the sidewalk restaurant.
You have the sidewalks, like any other city in the world. During the day, people walk on them. Not too much or you die because of the smog. When we get into the rush hours to move within the city is pretty much impossible. Then, at around 9.00 p.m. everything changes. The Chinese restaurant gang arrives. The kitchen on wheel is stored in an alley nearby and it is pushed by the son. The other son with the daughter arrive with the yellow pick-up, containing tables, ingredients, everything you can possibly need and/or imagine.
The father is in charge to settle things with the policeman (some informal 'tax' is paid to him), the water & electricity come from the shop on the street.
On the street you can buy everything. If there is something they don't have (like alcohol, cigarettes, whisky…) you simply walk into the Seven/Eleven and you get what you need.
By three, four, the business is over.
All the family members start to clean, wash, water.
In about 20 minutes, half of an hour, everything is gone.

Business datas?
Let's say 8 tables, 6 seats per table. An average of 300/400 customers per night. Each of them spend an average of 1 dollar per dinner.
300/400 dollars per night. 100 dollars go for the food. 25 dollars for wages (waitresses, the cook…), bribes, various expense. Net profit of about 200, 250 dollars per night. Since they work every single night, you get 6,000/7,500 US$ per month. In the city where if you work as a clerk in the post-office you get 250 US$ per month. Not bad, eh? This is the way the Chinese family system works, my friend. As Deng Xiao Ping once said, I don't care if the cat is black or white as long as he can catch the mice…

By four a.m., nothing is there. The city is now half asleep, ready to start again the whole process in few hours.

Illustrated by Superlover: Piaypong Bhumichitra, Chuti Srisanguanvilas

7-11 supermarket

street vender

7:00 a.m. - 3.00 p.m. Normal traffic. The road is a road, and the sidewalk is a sidewalk.

3.45 a.m. - 7.00 a.m. The city is vaguely asleep. The sidewalk is a sidewalk again.

the only thing still running is the 7-11!

the sidewalk now is perfectly clean!

3.00 p.m. - 9.00 p.m. Traffic jam time. Cars everywhere. To commute is impossible.

9.00 p.m.- 9.15 p.m. The transformation starts. The sidewalk becomes a restaurant.

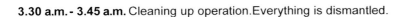

3.30 a.m. - 3.45 a.m. Cleaning up operation. Everything is dismantled.

9.15 p.m. - 3.30 a.m. The restaurant at its full steam.

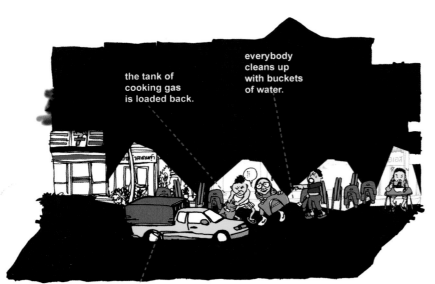

LOTA 2782

333

743
HERNANDO DE AGUIRRE

433

CARLOS ANTUNEZ
2841

Art 25:   Enclosures must be
100/ transparent towards the
street. public spaces in general
and between properties or
whenever possible not exist at
all.

352

CARMEN SYLVA
2669

AV. EL BOSQUE
276

310

261

LOTA
2635

THAYER OJEDA
300

Art. 28:   In residential
buildings. it will be compulsory
to provide 7 square meters of
open space per inhabitant.

NO PISAR
PASTO

222
HERNANDO DE AGUIRRE

FABRIZIO GALLANTI AND FRANCISCA INSULZA | SANTIAGO DE CHILE | MINI LANDSCAPES

Art. 30:   Any existing valuable trees on sidewalks or within lots must be maintained by future constructions.

minilandscapes. santiago de chile

SANDI HILAL AND ALESSANDRO PETTI

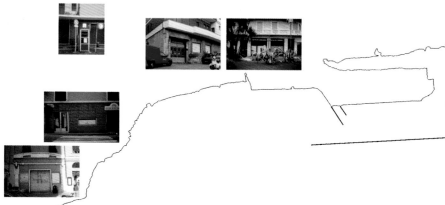

November 12, 1972, in Genoa there were 85 movie screens: 4 dedicated to *auteurs*, 14 to first runs, 7 to reruns of classics, 7 to delayed first runs, 22 to art-house, 31 to revivals and film festivals. A considerable number when compared to the 49 screens concentrated into Genoa's 24 movie theaters today, of which 26 screens are found in 2 multiplexes (identified with a * on map). These figures indicate a profound change not only in how entertainment is enjoyed, but also in the city's urban makeup. Each neighborhood before had a cinema but today that's no longer the case. What happened to these spaces? What have they become? What have replaced these places of spectacle and socialization? Some remain, yet others have been converted into supermarkets, banks, department stores, parking lots, gyms, etc.

Keeping these questions in mind, Project "12.11.1972" (courtesy of Pinksummer) uses a narrative device which chronicles the changes in Genoa's urban landscape, and more generally, that of the contemporary city. Like a time machine, it documents present and past. It shows the physical changes of those buildings that now host films and recalls the stories of those which on November 12, 1972 were still places of entertainment. The work is divided into 3 sections: slides, maps, and images. The first pairs of photographs of the theaters as seen today with a newspaper's film listings from November 12, 1972. The second picks out the location of the cinemas and provides historical and technical facts relevant to each. The third part is a montage of film clips with a soundtrack from one of the film's that now screens in a multiplex.

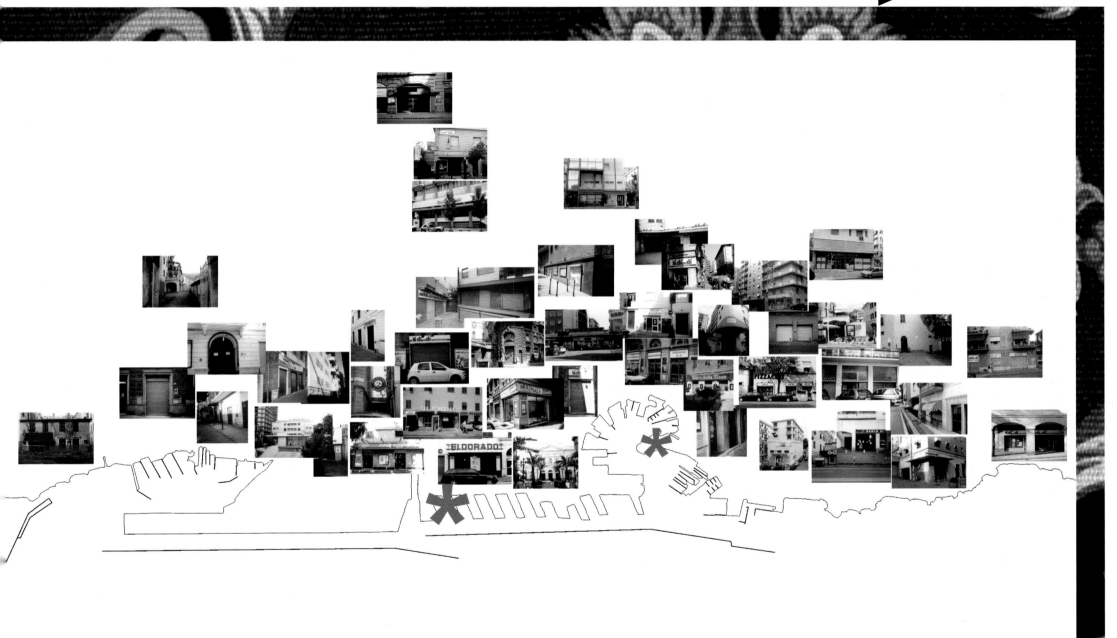

James Chong is managing director of "Challenge Manufactoring Pty. Ltd." and Immediate Past President of the "Chung Wah Association" in Western Australia: "My family moved from China to Malaysia, where it used to run a small coconut and rice plantation. I have two older brothers and three sisters, and I'm the youngest of the family. After my studies I worked there for a few years."

Sally Ng is the owner of "Canningvale Market Seafood": "I was born in Australia. But my family comes from Singapore, doing fishbowls and fishcakes. My uncle lives there and drives an important business. he supplies now internationally." Wei Chin Lee, together with his wife is the owner of "Spanow Indonesian restaurant": "I'm Chinese, born in

Saigon. Before I was a professional singer. Television, concerts...Then I had to join the soldiers. All was very difficult, because we were forced to fight the enemy." James Chong: "I saved a few dollars, and I decided to come to Australia for further education. I finished my degree in 1974. I found that Australia was a nice place to live in. My wife and myself decided to

stay in Perth. I started working, bought a house, became father. Finally, I set up my own business. I am now the head of a manufacturing factory located in the Perth suburbs." Sally Ng: "After I finished studying in Australia, I met my husband. We got married. I decided to learn how to make fishbowls and fishcakes. I asked my mother to show me how to make them.

In 1991 I started by myself a one person business in Australia." Wei Chin Lee: "Communist occupation forced me to leave the country. I stayed in a very small boat, with no water, no food. Only three ice-cubes each day per person to keep us alive. After three days and nights at sea, we were brought to a very big refugee camp in Indonesia. Already after four months, I was allowed

to immigrate to Australia. In Australia I got married. My wife is Chinese from Indonesia. Because she spoke a very poor English she could not find a job. But she is a very good cook. So we decided to open a very small business. Today we own a famous restaurant in Perth, where we do Indonesian house-style cooking." James Chong: "In Malaysia we stayed in a wooden house. My brother had built everything from scratch. A very simple, practical, large house, with six bedrooms upstairs and a very big kitchen. Because we had a very large family, and because everybody lived there, we needed three tables and had a big pot of rice. Once in Australia, I first lived in a very small house. I liked the place. It was very quiet, cheap and the plot was large. A sort of rental house, but not that bad. So I spent

some time to make it presentable. We lived there for a few years. When the house became too small, I decided to subdivide the land and build my second house. That is where we are living now: near the golf-course, because I like to play golf. In our street we are the only Chinese family. My factory is distant almost thirty minutes drive from my house. The factory employ few people.

My partner is Spanish. Many of the employees are Asian, because they are good and reliable workers."

Sally Ng: " At the beginning of my business, I worked at home, in my private kitchen. The kitchen was a domestic kitchen, very small. I made all fishbowls by my own hands, because I sold them only once a week on the market. Today, since the business is much bigger, I have

got a warehouse, that has a total capacity of five hundred kilos of stock. I only employ five people, plus my family. All together ten people."

Wei Chin Lee: "I could have had a business like this in my own country, because people need to eat. Here, business is very tough. Taxes and wages are very high. And there's a lot of competition. When I started, just across

the street, in a very small place, Perth had four Indonesian restaurants altogether. Now there are more that forty. We are actually very lucky in our current space, because we pay a low rent. We know the previous tenants and the landlord. We do a lot of things for them. Still, my wife and myself, we have to work very hard, together with a few employees. Luckily we live just a ten minutes drive from

the restaurant. We have been residents in this neighbourhood for sixteen years. Our neighbours are very nice. I have never seen any of them behaving bad against Asians.

PERTH–The Chinese Connection
multiplicity
27 JAN - 3 FEB 2002

Fieldwork:	4days
Team:	Francesco Jodice, Maki Gherzi, John Palmesino, Carole Schmit
Consultants:	Sophie O'Brien, Christine Choo,
Interviews:	James Chong, Sally Ng, Wei Chin Lee
E-mails:	325
Maps:	19
Video footage:	6 hours
Photographs:	650
km travelled:	760

3876
CEDRIC PRICE
aka
HGWELLS
IF THEN WE REPRESENT OUR EARTH AS A LITTLE BALL OF ONE INCH
DIAMETER THEN THE SUN WOULD BE A BIG GLOBE NINE FEET ACROSS AND
323 YARDS AWAY
THAT IS ABOUT A FIFTH ON A MILE
FOUR OR FIVE MINUTES OF WALKING
OR
3876 CUPS OF COFFEE

Neutrality

22 MAR 2002
Final Report of the ICE Switzerland-Second WW

21 NOV 1921, Lausanne Treaty

17-18 MAY 1995
Israeli-Palestinian negotiations, Montreux

1-3 JUN 2003 G8 Summit in Evian

27-29 APR 1993, Israeli-Palestinian negotiations, Geneva
19-21 NOV 1985 Reagan-Gorbachev Summit
17 MAY 1954 Construction of CERN
18 MAR 2004 Protocol of Privileges and Immunities CERN
1 JAN 1995 World Trade Organization Established in Geneva
28-30 JAN 1985 73rd (Extraordinary) OPEC Conference
24 NOV 1959 First Acceleration of Protons CERN
15 NOV 1920 First League of the Nations General Meeting
7 APR 1948 Establishment of the World Health Organization
3 SEP 1962 Board of Governors, OPEC Headquarters
12-14 DEC 1995, Israeli-Palestinian negotiations, Geneva
22 AUG 1864 I Red Cross Convention
06 JUL 1906 II Red Cross Convention
17 JUL 1929 III Red Cross Convention
1977 IV Red Cross Convention
10-12 DEC 2003 World Summit on the Information Society

eneral Kofi Annan meets Cyprus leaders

JAN 1999
Clashes with No-Global
Landquart

29 JAN 2002 Israeli-Palestinian negotiations, Davos
WORLD ECONOMIC FORUM
Davos

24 OCT 2001
Incident in the Gotthard Tunnel
blocks continental traffic

5-6 OCT 1925, Locarno Treaty

26 JAN 2001, Chiasso

As we take a further step into the shards of contemporaneity, not to have a policy, not to stand for something, not to take part, not to participate, to be a-political is becoming more and more a difficult, contrasted, almost immoral condition. Yet these difficulties are also an entry point to the unveiling of the comeback of the physical condition, of the materic body of our contemporary territories. Neutrality is a way to correlate empirical observations of the transformation of space: international, local, urban, humanitarian, political, conflictual, economical, financial, military, institutional, global, individual. Neutrality is a specific way of organising matter in space in order to create an extra-territorial operational zone where to manage conflicts, contradictions, emergencies, diversities. Neutrality is a modality of creating a counterpart to the hierarchical understanding of geo-politics, of identity, of internationalism, of the nuances of peace and war in the wake of globalisation. To be neutral, in a certain sense and under certain circumstances, can be understood as the ultimate contemporary political and powerful condition. A condition that engages individuals with the spatial organisation of our institutions, our nations, our wars, our lives.

JP, ASR

Stalker: a travel through the becoming of the city of Rome (first published in *Suburban discipline*, Princeton Architectural Press, 1997). Rome is a city with 3.5 million of inhabitants and, at the same time, it is also the largest agricultural commune of Europe, it combines dimensions at a metropolitan scale, with a high flux density, together with vast open spaces, where one can encounter sheep grazing in fields crossed by Roman aqueducts, modern electrocutes, and nomad camps. A city that is rich of different conceptions of space and time, that are due to the nature of it's complex orography and consequence of the city's historical evolution. In over it's twothousand year history, the city has first expanded, then contract itself various times: from over a million of inhabitants in Imperial Rome, to less than a few thousand during the Middle Ages, to become today, a modern metropolis. Throughout this pulsing process the city has generated vast abandoned areas, though extremely rich in history and pregnant of future, they lack the dimension of present. 'Terrains Vagues' today a topical issue, have always been a peculiarity of this city. These spaces are today existing in all major modern cities, in such an evident manner that they have been Typologically individualised, but not everywhere they have reached such a morphological richness, and such an extensive and complicated presence as they have in the city of Rome, I believe that these areas offer the most interesting point of view of the high complexity of the city's nature, for those who intend to observe the evolution of modern metropolis. The laboratory for territorial researches: Stalker, explored these interstitial spaces of the city of Rome; from the 5th to the 9th of October 1995, the first journey through what we called 'Actual Territories,' empty spaces that are abandoned or in transformation. We covered about 70 kms on foot, camping in tents, without ever leaving the city, but never entering it properly either, through areas that are unknown and invisible to most, though they cover a vast territorial extension, maybe larger than the built city itself. We started our journey with the aim of returning to the starting point: the unemployed train station of Vigna Clara, after having crossed the entire city on self-created tracks, that had never been traced, travelling on it's negative side to witness it's existence, to perceive the city's autonomous evolution distant from the sight, and therefor from the control of man; we undertook this route especially to prove the rich articulation, the continuity and the deep penetration of these areas throughout the entire. Our travel took us to cross fences, railroad tracks, and highways, linking places that are now permanently disconnected, it also allowed us to discover new and huge distances between contiguous neighbourhoods, spending hours to cross areas that one connected in minutes by car. We travelled through different space-time dimensions during our journey. Our anxiety in entering spaces that lack a main door, tearing apart wire netting and climbing over walls, made our senses continuously alert, our movements cautious, the territorial cognition became reason of survival, restoring to our sight the capacity of observation. Through this experience we crossed a territory, and it's discovery became a creative statement. We realised a path who's continuos but at the same time tortuous and unexpected course, transformed in connections the chaotic and casual relations that occur between nature and the discarded human waste, that combining themselves in a process of mutual transformation, distinguish these spaces. We travelled through the past and the future of the city, through it's lost memories, and it's unconscious becoming, in a territory created by mankind, above his will. In this void we designed an ephemeral subjective geography, instantaneous statements of a world in constant transformation: in fact, we created a space without having planned or built it, by simply crossing it. This makes our experience an 'architectural practice'. This is because we believe that: 'the space that belongs to architecture is not a geometrical and individualised place, it is not the ideal projection of the human thought nor container of our being-in-the-world, but in daily reality, it's our same being-in-the-world that is invisible and undistinguished.'[1] Today more and more architects work on the marginal grounds of the discipline, behaviour that doesn't escape from architecture, but it expresses the desire to contaminate architecture itself. This contamination evolves through the creation of new and paradigmatic 'containers' of architecture, through the realisation of a path, an existentialist practice, that consents to mature the consciousness of the world's becoming and of our taking part in evolution. 'Plan behaviours instead of formal volumeters, both when imposed by political power, or when inherited from custom or from the modern tradition. One must tend to a society without a father, one must be able to desume spatial qualities and behaviours from that right of autodetermination, that does not consent to delegate under any form. To aim for the compelling need to verify scientifically proven conjectures on space, to be able to combine the revolution of architecture to the struggle for the transformation of the political structures. In conclusion, the goal is the creation of a passage from a formalistic idea of space to the reality of the daily experienced space.'[2] During the creation of the map of our journey, we felt the need to represent the city as a planet, we coated a sphere with the plan of the city, distinguishing the built part of the city, densely populated, in yellow, the same colour that is used to represent the earth in geographical atlases, and blue, the colour of oceans and seas, for the empty spaces. The route we took throughout our journey is marked by a white line, uncertain and shaky in the midst of that blue. The morphology of the city, filtered through those two colours, was an excellent manner to visualise the geography of a planet, covered mostly by water, with it's continents drifted apart, a cluster of islands spread out at sea. Given the world, through modern technologies, is evolving into a global village, in which the huge distances have disappeared because of the growing speed of the connective net-work, it is also true that the city, through the fractures and the separations generated by those same systems, has become the environment where one can encounter new spaces and insurmountable distances. The voids in the urban context, in a similar fashion as in oceans, are crossed by rapid connecting ways, beneath which deep and unexplored worlds are hidden. That blue we used was nothing more than the background on which the city's outline stands out. The relation between the background and the figure itself 'consists in recognising the background as an active generator of visual energy, that balances the strength of the figures, assuming therefor a positive role. In such a manner that the background itself becomes a figure. The negative space recognises the active function of what can no longer be considered as an interposed void."[3] The press coverage of our journey in the media environment was quite unexpected, in consideration of the fact that it was quite an elusive operation, marginal and difficult to define, accomplished by a group of mostly young architects together with artists and scientific researchers, struck by a sudden childish behaviour, and with enough free time to spend. There was a first article, the day we started out, it was published on a left-wing, slightly intellectual newspaper, who contacted us at our return for a second article which also featured our address. Since then we have been contacted by anthropologists, philosophers, sociologists, art critics, and even by a fashion magazine, and by a television production, finally, in the end, an architectural magazine, that was not Italian but French, published an article about us. We started to travel through a different archipelago, not made out of built up islands, but formed by isolated worlds, where different disciplines configure themselves autonomously through their own communication systems. This immaterial world that bears the same characteristics of the global village, where the huge communication highways tend to transform into homogeneous and bland, the relations between these various islands, that anyway maintain their qualities of self-reference and of reciprocal indifference. Here we find more and more, vast and deep voids, territories able to contain huge distances, new and infinite spaces that are meant to be crossed without a precise aim, but with a nomad and observing attitude, that John Keats called 'negative capacity' that enables to 'place oneself in a state of doubt, of mystery, surrounded by darkness, without pursuing that irritating need of facts and reasons,' and that 'involves a knowledge that can not be obtained through defeat, but through being attentive, and through the contemplation of differences.'[4]

Footnotes
1. Cesare Brandi, *La spazialità antiprospettica*, in Bruno Zevi, *Architettura, concetti di una controstoria*, Rome: 1994, p. 74
2. Aldo Loris Rossi and D. Mazzoleni, *Spazio e comportamento*, in Bruno Zevi, *Ibidem*, p. 72
3. Rudolph Arnheim, *Spazio negativo in architettura*, in Bruno Zevi, *Ibidem*.
4. Richard Sennet, *The conscience of the eye*, New York: 1990 p. 270.

Lorenzo Romito for Stalker

TOROLAB
TIJUANA

UNITED STATES
SAN DIEGO

TIJUANA
MEXICO

TO LOS ANGELES

What is it we want when there's the need for basic infrastructure only on one side of two overlapped city grids divided with a political border?

Under this context the reality of the permeable frontier/border and Auge's "Zero Space" only appear evident as a relief of a city that was never built, so Debord's "Ludic Preoccupations" become not only absent but also extinct as the necessity for survival replaces social relation with urban camouflage and the transitory constructions that replace the notion of neighborhoods with an ephemeral loop that becomes permanent.

This can only be answered with "Emergency Architecture", so our need doesn't have to be conciliated with our desires.

significant routes / personal roads
cognitive cartography / landmarks
situation map / events

95% are unpaved roads

lagunitas

site   industrial pacifico II

la gloria

el tecolote

la jolla

05 minutes walking

15 minutes walking

30 minutes walking

ejido lázaro cárdenas

TO ENSENADA

This is the mapping of our "9 Families (minus one)" project.
This Architecture has the distinctive features that architects are needed as facilitators not designers and that it follows the consumption flow of recuperated materials to construct not architectural forms, but transpersonal structures to enhance quality of life.

Artway of thinking Founded in 1992 by Italian artists Stefania Mantovani and Federica Thiene. All of their projects are conceived jointly and count on the active participation of the communities they focus on. These artists' main concerns revolve around culture, socioeconomics, and both urban and natural landscapes. For Mantovani and Thiene, the challenge lies in being able to construct 'hybrid projections,' that is, common codes for people of diverse backgrounds and careers. They see art precisely as a daily practice in all areas of life, i.e., as a series of innovative ways of thinking, imagining, behaving, and relating to others.

Stefano Boeri (Milan 1956) is an architect and urban planner. Since January 2004 he has been the director of *Domus*, and he contributes regularly to the cultural pages of *Il Sole 24 Ore*, the main Italian economic newspaper. His research centers around the interface of architecture and urbanism with a focus on new conditions for European City. His office studio (Boeri Studio; shared with Gianandrea Barreca and Giovanni La Varra) is involved in many transformation projects in port areas in the Mediterranean region (Genoa, Naples, Mytilene, Salerno, Trieste). He is a Founding member of Multiplicity, a research agency concerned with the state of urban living through which he has promoted a series of research projects and installations. He is also co-author of: Multiplicity, *USE*, Milan: Skira 2003. Various authors, *Mutations*, Barcelona: Actar 2000. G. Basilico, S. Boeri, *Italy: Cross Sections of a Country*, Zurich: Scalo 1998.

Rachaporn Choochuey and Stefano Mirti Rachaporn Choochuey is an architect, currently lives and works in Bangkok. She received her degrees in Architecture from Chulalongkorn University, Bangkok and Columbia University, New York and a Ph.D. from The University of Tokyo. Since 2002 she has been a lecturer in the Faculty of Architecture, Chulalongkorn University. ⏐Stefano Mirti is an architect who has worked in Italy, Tokyo, Seoul, Bangkok. He received his Ph.D. in Architecture from the Politecnico di Torino, Turin, Italy (1998) with a thesis on the architects Charles Eames and Franco Albini. He is a founder and a member of Cliostraat. Since 2001 he has been an associate professor of Interaction Design Institute, Ivrea.

Fabrizio Gallanti and Francisca Insulza Fabrizio Gallanti (Genoa, 1969). Architect, University of Genoa, and Ph.D. in architectural design from the Politecnico di Torino. Since 1993 he has been a founding member of Gruppo A12. In 1997 he won the Akademie Solitude Fellowship, Stuttgart (Germany) of which he was nominated president of the Jury in 2001 and 2003. From 1998 to 2000 he worked as a curator at the Milan Triennale (Italy) and in 2001 won the Canon Foundation Research Fellowship, Tokyo (Japan). At present he lives in Santiago, Chile, practicing as an architect and teaching architectural design and architectural theory at the Pontificia Universidad Católica de Chile and Universidad Diego Portales. He writes for international magazines such as *Purple*, *Abitare*, *Domus* and *32*. ⏐Francisca Insulza Ambrosio (Ann Arbor, US, 1970). Architect, Universidad Central de Chile and Master of Architecture, Berlage Institute, Rotterdam. Since 1998 she has taught and carried out research in Chile and abroad (Berlage Institute, Rotterdam, Pontificia Universidad Católica de Chile, Universidad Diego Portales). Founding member of Multiplicity, she has participated in research projects concerning territorial transformation and the representation of urban dynamics including USE Uncertain States of Europe and Solid Sea. She has published articles in *Hunch*, *Domus* and *Architektur Aktuell* and participated in various publications including *Mutations* (Barcelona: Actar 2000) and *USE-Uncertain Sates of Europe* (Milan: Skira 2003).

Sandi Hilal and Alessandro Petti (www.statelessnation.org) Sandi Hilal (Bethlehem 1973) is an architect and urban planner, she carries out research activity primarily on 'transborder policies for daily life' at the University of Trieste. ⏐Alessandro Petti (Pescara 1973) is an architect and urban planner. He is a researcher in urban planning at the university of architecture in Venice. Their project 'statelessnation' was invited to the 50th Biennale di Venezia.

Gruppo A12 (Nicoletta Artuso, Andrea Balestrero, Gianandrea Barreca, Antonella Bruzzese, Maddalena De Ferrari, Fabrizio Gallanti, Massimiliano Marchica). Gruppo A12 is a collective structure team born in Genoa in 1993, based in Genoa and Milan. The activities of the group are focused on the themes of architecture, urbanism and contemporary arts. Three fields that Gruppo A12 tries to connect working on architectural and urban projects (international architecture competition 'Europan 5' Biel, Switzerland, first prize) are: art installations ('empty/Sumi', Manifesta 3, Ljubljana, 2000; the temporary Italian pavillion 'La Zona' 50th Intl. Art Exhibition Venice Biennal, 2003); urban interventions ('Epidemie urbane', Biennale dei giovani artisti del Mediterraneo, Turin, 1997); and exhibition and research projects ('N 33° 51' E 130° 47" Center for Contemporary Arts, Kitakyushu, Japan, 2002), which mixes various knowledges expertise, tools and attitudes.

Armin Linke was born in 1966 and lives in Milan. As a photographer and filmmaker he is working on an ongoing archive about human activity and the most varied natural and man-made landscapes. He tries to document scenes where the boundary between fiction and non-fiction blurs or becomes invisible. Among his publications: *Transient*, Milan Skira 2003. *4Flight*, Milan: a+mbookstore 2002. *Portrait*, Milan: a+mbookstore 1999. *1048*, Milan: a+mbookstore 1998. *Instant Book, 1/2/3*, Milan: a+mbookstore 1996. *Dell'Arte nei volti*, Milan: Federico Motta Editore 1994.

Multiplicity (Stefano Boeri, Maddalena Bregani, Maki Gherzi, Matteo Ghidoni, Francisca Insulza, Francesco Jodice, Giovanni Lavarra, John Palmesino) Multiplicity is an agency for territorial investigations based in Milan. The agency realizes projects in different areas of the world using multiple systems of analysis, surveying and representation. Multiplicity is an ever-changing network (involving up to 80 persons) recruited in the actual geographical area of intervention. The network is formed by architects, geographers, artists, photographers, sociologists, journalists, economists, filmmakers etc. Multiplicity produces installations, workshops and books about the recent and hidden processes of transformation of the urban condition. Multiplicity detects the physical environment, researching clues and traces produced by new social behaviours. Among the projects: *USE-Uncertain State of Europe* (Mutations, Bordeaux, 2000), *Tokyo Voids* (Void, Rice Gallery, Tokyo, 2002), *Solid Sea* (Documenta 11, Kassel, 2002), *Border Device* (50th Biennale di Venezia, Venice).

Hans Ulrich Obrist and Cedric Price Hans Ulrich Obrist has curated exhibitions at the Musée d'Art Moderne de la Ville de Paris; the Kunsthalle, Wien; Deichtor-Hallen, Hamburg; and Serpentine Gallery in London, among other institutions. He currently divides his time between France, Switzerland and Austria. After an initial training in economics and politics, he switched to contemporary art and has organised a variety of exhibitions in such unlikely venues as his own house, a monastery library, an airplane and a hotel. Among his most important publications are: *World soup*, Munich: 1993; *Delta X*, Regensburg: 1996; *Unbuilt roads: 107 unrealized projects*, Ostfildern: 1997; *Vito Acconci im Gespräch mit Hans-Ulrich Obrist*, 1993; *Text: Schriften und Interviews / Gerhard Richter* [ed.], Frankfurt am Main: 1993; *Félix González-Torres im Gespräch mit Hans-Ulrich Obrist*, 1994; *Bertrand Lavier: Argo* [ed.], 1994; *Dara Birnbaum im Gespräch mit Hans-Ulrich Obrist*, 1995; *Christian Boltanski im Gespräch mit Hans-Ulrich Obrist*, 1995; *Annette Messager. Nos témoignages*, 1995; *Lost day : 1972 / Gilbert & George* [ed.], Cologne: 1996; *Laboratorium* [with Barbara Vanderlinden, ed.s], Antwerpen: 1999. *Interviste*, volume 1, Milan: Charta 2003. Cedric Price founded Cedric Price Architects, London, in 1960 and began his practice with an aviary for London Zoo, designed in 1961 with Lord Snowdon and Frank Newby. Among his other realized projects are the Inter-Action Trust Community Centre, Kentish Town, London; the Olympic Information Complex for the Munich Olympic Village; Stratford Railway Station; and Dockland Development for Hamburg, Germany. Price's reputation and influence rest chiefly, however, on the radicalism of his ideas. Among his highly original proposals are the Fun Palace in London; the Potteries Thinkbelt Project, which imagined the re-use of an abandoned railway line for a roving university located in the train carriages; and the Trondheim Student Centre Project (with Archigram Architects). Characteristically, Price argues against the production of permanent, specific spaces for particular functions, stressing instead the need for flexibility and the unpredictability of future use. He has consistently defended the importance of modern technologies in architectural design and construction. At the same time, he seeks to analyze the specific motivations that might give rise to a structure in the first place. 'Technology is the answer,' he has said, 'but what was the question?' Cedric Price received his undergraduate degree in architecture from Cambridge University in 1955 and his diploma from the Architectural Association in London in 1957. His work has been published in many journals and modern architectural histories.

John Palmesino with Ann-Sofi Rönnskog John Palmesino (Switzerland, 1970). Founding member of Multiplicity, Milan, Italy. Head of research, ETH Studio Basel – Contemporary City Institute, Basel, Switzerland. Co-author of *USE Uncertain states of Europe*, Milan: Skira 2003. Co-author of *Lessico Postfordista. Dizionario di idee della mutazione*, Milan: Feltrinelli 2000. His researches focus on the transformation processes of the contemporary urban territories. Current projects include: INERTIA – A series of portraits of cities in the shadow of globalisation (Naples, Detroit, Hong Kong, Paris, St Petersburg) and NEUTRALITY, an inquiry into the contemporary international, political, urban, infrastructural, humanitarian and individual conditions of extra-territoriality. Ann-Sofi Rönnskog (Finland, 1976). Architect. Studies in Oulu, Copenhagen, Zürich, Helsinki. Focus in urbanism. Research Assistant, ETH Studio Basel – Contemporary City Institute, Basel, Switzerland. Current project 'Die Schweiz- ein städtebauliches Portrait'.

Stalker is a collective subject group that engages conducts research and actions within the landscape, paying particular attention to the areas around the city's margins and forgotten urban space, and abandoned areas or regions under transformation. Stalker is at once custodian, guide and artist for these 'Actual Territories.' Since May 1999, Stalker, with the Kurdish community of Rome, has taken over and occupied a building in Campo Boario (former slaughter house) in order to experiment a new shape form of contemporary public-space, based on the acceptance, hospitality, and the relationship between the artistic activity and the civil solidarity. The building has been renamed 'Ararat', in order to be a hope for the people in exile and a public space that constitutes wealth for the whole entire city. Stalker means to inquire alternative possibilities to the traditional modalities of city participation, through actions, plans, competitions, exhibitions, workshops and various shapes of mapping and recycling of territory developed, in 2002, by a newly-formed, multidisciplinary research lab, 'Osservatorio Nomade.'

Torolab is a Tijuana-based consortium of artists, designers and musicians. It was founded in 1995 by architect and artist Raúl Cárdenas Osuna as a socially engaged 'laboratory' and is committed to residents of Tijuana and the entire trans-border region. Among their projects is ToroVestimenta, a clothing line that equips for the hostile border environment. The multi-pocketed Transborder Pants, for example, provide not only a perfect fit for a Mexican passport, but also draw attention to this social reality.

Francesco Jodice

1967	Born in Naples; currently lives in Milan.
1995	Starts to work with photography, film, maps and writings.
1996	Graduates as architect.
2000	Founding member of Multiplicity, an international network of artists and architects.
	Among Multiplicity projects: *Tokyo Voids*; *USE: Uncertain States of Europe*; *Solid Sea*.
2004	Named Professor of Theory and Practice of the technological image, Faculty of Design and Art, University of Bolzano, Italy.

Major Projects

1997 (ongoing)	*What We Want*. An atlas of social and urban behaviours through fifty world metropolis.
1998 (ongoing)	*The Secret Traces*. A research based on the photographic shadowing of unknown people in several cities across the globe.
	Observing and comparing the lifestyle of anonymous citizens through their daily routines.
2000 (ongoing)	*100 Stories*. One hundred short photo-animations of unaware people spied on while doing meaningless gestures.
2002 (ongoing)	*Natura*. A series of case studies reconstructing criminal or bizarre events that took place in various rural areas around the world. Among which
	The Crandell Case (upstate New York, August 2002), and *Il caso Monte Maggiore* (Caserta, June 2003).
2003	*The Gift*. Co-directed and wrote with Sebastiano Jodice a 35 mm short film.

Selected Solo Exhibitions

2004	*Private Investigations*, Mudimadue Gallery, Berlin
2003	*What We Want*, Galería Marta Cervera, Madrid
2003	*The Crandell Case*, Photo & Contemporary, Turin
2003	*The Random Viewer*, Galleria Spazio Erasmus, Milan

Selected Group Exhibitions

2003	*Il caso Monte Maggiore*, IN-Natura, X Biennale Internazionale di Fotografia, Turin
2003	*Border Device* (Multiplicity), 50 Biennale di Venezia, Venice
2003	*100 Stories*, XIV Quadriennale di Roma, Naples
2002	*Solid Sea* (Multiplicity), DOCUMENTA 11, Kassel
2002	*Tokyo Voids* (Multiplicity), VOID, Rice Gallery/G2, Tokyo
2002	*The Secret Traces*, Side Effects, Triennale di Milano, Milan
2002	*The Crandell Case*, Artomi, Omi, New York
2001	*What We Want*, Instant city, Museo Pecci, Prato
2000	*USE: Uncertain States of Europe* (Multiplicity), Mutations, Bordeaux

Selected Bibliography

2003	*USE: Uncertain States of Europe*, (Multiplicity), Milan: Skira
2002	Various authors, *Side Effects*, Milan: Silvana Editoriale
2001	Various authors, *Instant City*, Milan: Baldini & Castoldi
2000	Various authors, *Mutations*, Barcelona: Actar
1998	*Cartoline dagli altri spazi*, Milan: Federico Motta editore

www.francescojodice.com   **www.multiplicity.it**